Light and shadows

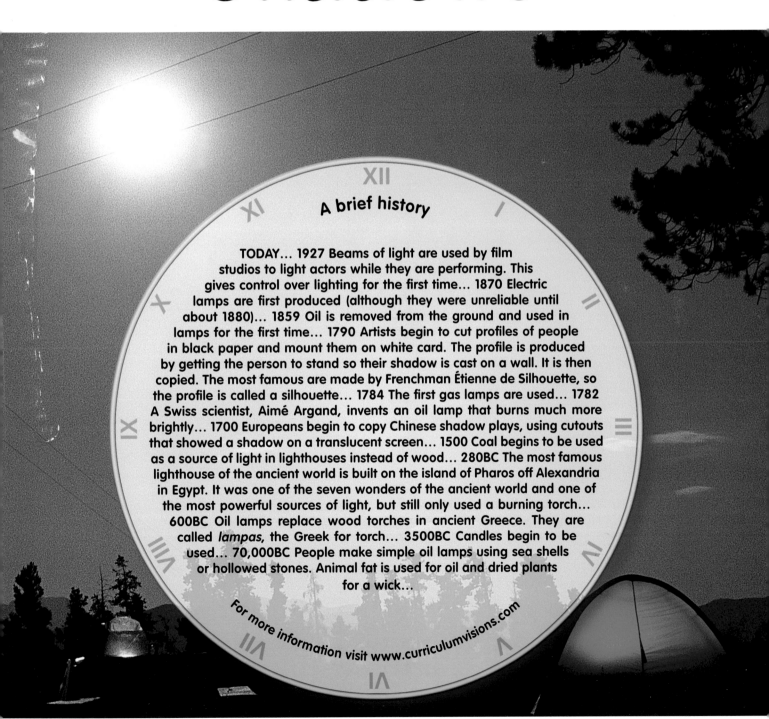

A brief history

TODAY... 1927 Beams of light are used by film studios to light actors while they are performing. This gives control over lighting for the first time... 1870 Electric lamps are first produced (although they were unreliable until about 1880)... 1859 Oil is removed from the ground and used in lamps for the first time... 1790 Artists begin to cut profiles of people in black paper and mount them on white card. The profile is produced by getting the person to stand so their shadow is cast on a wall. It is then copied. The most famous are made by Frenchman Étienne de Silhouette, so the profile is called a silhouette... 1784 The first gas lamps are used... 1782 A Swiss scientist, Aimé Argand, invents an oil lamp that burns much more brightly... 1700 Europeans begin to copy Chinese shadow plays, using cutouts that showed a shadow on a translucent screen... 1500 Coal begins to be used as a source of light in lighthouses instead of wood... 280BC The most famous lighthouse of the ancient world is built on the island of Pharos off Alexandria in Egypt. It was one of the seven wonders of the ancient world and one of the most powerful sources of light, but still only used a burning torch... 600BC Oil lamps replace wood torches in ancient Greece. They are called *lampas*, the Greek for torch... 3500BC Candles begin to be used... 70,000BC People make simple oil lamps using sea shells or hollowed stones. Animal fat is used for oil and dried plants for a wick...

For more information visit www.curriculumvisions.com

Dr Brian Knapp

Word list

These are some science words that you should look out for as you go through the book. They are shown using CAPITAL letters.

BEAM
A broad band or shaft of light, such as that produced by a torch. Sunbeams are beams of sunlight.

FILTER
A transparent or translucent material, usually glass or plastic, that blocks out only part of the light. For example, a red glass is a filter because it blocks all of the light except red.

ILLUMINATED
Brightly lit.

OPAQUE
Something that light cannot get through. Opposite of transparent. Plastics, wood and metals are all opaque materials.

REFLECTION
When light is bounced from a surface, such as by lightly-coloured card or shiny foil.

SHADE
A place that does not get direct sunlight because something, for example, a tree, is blocking out the direct light from the Sun.

SHADOW
A dark shape that is cast by an object on to the ground or a wall. Shadows are evenly dark and have no detail. As a result, no matter how complicated the shape, only the edge of the shadow will have any detail.

SILHOUETTE
The black outline of an object when seen from its shadow.

SOURCE OF LIGHT
Something that gives out light. The Sun and other stars are the largest sources of light. Street lights, fires, oil and gas lamps and torches are other examples of sources of light.

STAINED GLASS WINDOW
Window glass that has colours on its surface. The colours filter the light so that stained glass is often beautifully coloured.

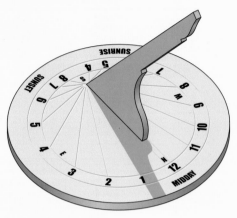

SUNDIAL
A device that uses sunlight to measure the time. As the Sun travels across the sky each day, the shadow it casts travels around a dial. The dial is marked in hours. Sundials can only tell time during the daylight, and are practically useless on a cloudy day because there is no clear shadow.

TRANSLUCENT
A material that will let some light through, but not enough for you to be able to see through it. Greaseproof paper is an example of translucent paper.

TRANSPARENT
Something that light will pass through easily. Opposite of opaque. Glass is a common transparent material.

Weblink: www.curriculumvisions.com

Contents

(Teachers should note that the apparent movement of the Sun in the sky is covered in the *Science@School* title *5E Earth and beyond*)

Weblink: www.curriculumvisions.com

Sunlight

Our main SOURCE OF LIGHT is the Sun. Its light reaches us even when it is cloudy.

▲ **(Picture 1) The Sun is our main source of light.**

⚠ **WARNING** Never look directly at the Sun. It can damage your eyes.

We see things because of light. Without light we can see nothing at all.

The rules for bright light

Light comes from anything that shines (Picture 1). But not everything gives us the same amount of light.

For light to be bright you need one or more of these:

▶ The light must be strong.
▶ The light source must be big.
▶ The light source must be close.

So, the brighter a light shines, the bigger it is, and/or the closer it is, the more it can light our world.

4

Torchlight and sunlight

If you look straight at a torchlight bulb you may be dazzled and think the light is very powerful.

Look at a torchlight in a darkened room. The source of the light is the tiny bulb in its centre. Although it is very bright, the bulb is so tiny that it can never light a whole room. It can only light things that are very close to it (Picture 2).

Pull back the curtains. Look at the light from a torch bulb again. Its light is hard to see. This tells us that daylight is far brighter than torchlight.

▲ (Picture 2) A torch is a useful, but weak, source of light.

Daylight is sunlight

Daylight comes from the Sun (Picture 3). Although it is far away, the Sun is very, very big and its light is very strong. This is why it would hurt our eyes if we looked straight at it.

Sunlight is so powerful that light can get right through even thick clouds.

◀ (Picture 3) This is the Sun seen through a powerful telescope. The dark and light areas show where the surface gases are boiling.

 What do you need if a light is to be bright?

Summary
- The Sun is the most powerful source of light in our world.
- It gives out light because it is bright and huge.

Weblink: www.curriculumvisions.com

Indoor lighting

We use many different sources of light for the times when it is dark.

The largest source of light is the Sun. But the Sun only shines during the day. Since ancient times, therefore, people have tried to make light for themselves so that they could see at night (Picture 1).

▼ (Picture 1) For thousands of years fire was the main source of light at night-time. These torches were made of bundles of rushes dipped in fat.

▼ (Picture 2) Candles were easier to use than oil lamps because their source of fuel was a solid wax, but they still gave out weak light.

▼ (Picture 3) This is an oil lamp made from a hollowed-out stone. A wick was placed in the oil in the bowl and then lit to give hours of light.

Artificial light

The earliest kinds of light were made by people burning wood or dried grasses. They used open fires and also tied bundles of reeds together to make a 'torch'. Then oil lamps and, later, candles were invented (Pictures 2 and 3). These burned oil and fat from animals.

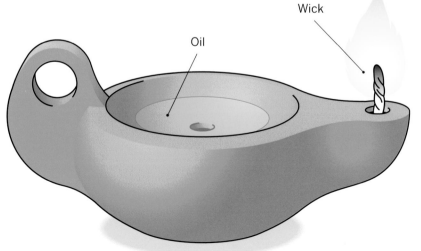

Wick

Oil

Weblink: www.curriculumvisions.com

Electric light

Sunlight

Candlelight

Firelight

▲ (Picture 4) Sources of light in a modern home (as well as sunlight through the windows) include light from electric lamps and light from a fire. In the past, there was no electricity and so light would have come from a gas or oil lamp or a candle. These were not as bright as modern electric lights.

Eventually, gas light and then electric light were invented, and for the first time people could have homes lit brightly enough to be able to read or work at night (Picture 4).

Modern light

You can get a good idea of how little light we can make for ourselves if you turn on all of the lights in a room on a bright sunny day. You will find they make almost no difference.

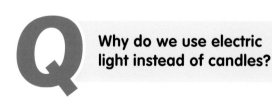

Q Why do we use electric light instead of candles?

Summary
• We use artificial light to help us see indoors and at night.
• Artificial light is much weaker than sunlight.

Weblink: www.curriculumvisions.com

Outdoor lighting

We can only light very small parts of the world around us at night.

We can light our homes and schools quite well because these are only small places. But when we try outside lighting, we find out how difficult it is to turn night into day.

The only natural light at night comes from the Moon (Picture 1). The Moon has no light of its own; it is simply bouncing off light it gets from the Sun.

The most powerful outdoor lights that we can make are used in football stadiums and other places where important competitions are taking place.

▲ (Picture 1) The Moon is the major source of light on many nights in the countryside.

The cost of bright lighting is high. If you look along a street at night you will see the lighting we have for our cities is only just enough to see by (Picture 2).

▼ (Picture 2) Street lighting is really not very bright. That is why cars have to have their own lights.

Weblink: www.curriculumvisions.com

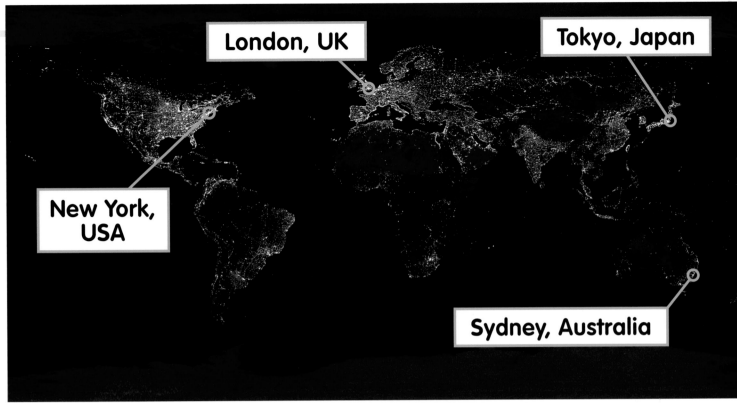

London, UK

Tokyo, Japan

New York, USA

Sydney, Australia

▲▶ (Pictures 3 and 4) The top picture shows the lights of the world's cities as seen from space. Even the lights in the world's brightest cities, such as New York (bottom right), are not powerful enough to turn night into day.

How we light our world

You can get a good idea of how little light we can make for ourselves if you look at our world from space at night (Pictures 3 and 4). As you can see, we only manage to light up tiny patches of the world. The rest – the countryside and oceans – stays dark.

 Why do we need car headlamps?

Summary
- We use street lights to help us see outdoors at night.
- We can only light up small parts of our world at night.

Weblink: www.curriculumvisions.com

Beams of light

Light travels in straight lines and cannot curve around things.

Street lights do not light anything very brightly. If we want to make something brighter, we need to narrow the light and send it in just one direction. Car headlamps are like this (Picture 1). We call the light from a headlamp a **BEAM** of light.

A beam of light is usually invisible. To see it, there has to be something to 'catch' the light. The water droplets in fog can catch the light and show how a beam of light spreads out (Picture 2).

As the light shines out from the headlamps, it catches the tiny droplets of fog and they shine, too.

▲ (Picture 1) At night we see headlamps and the road they are shining on. But we do not usually see the light beam itself.

▼ (Picture 2) You can see a beam of light when it is foggy.

Weblink: www.curriculumvisions.com

(Picture 3) Light beams can be seen in an early morning mist. In this case the beams of light have been caught by the tiny droplets of water in the mist, and we see them sparkling as light falls on them.

Beams of light can also be seen in the early morning mist (Picture 3).

In both cases, we can see how the edges of the beams of light are straight. This shows us that light moves in straight lines.

(Picture 4) Rays of light can be made by cutting thin slits in a piece of cardboard. The torch beam will show in a darkened room.

Q When do we see the path of a beam of light?

Light travels through slits

There is one other easy way in which we can see beams of light indoors. If we cut thin slits in a piece of card and then shine a torch at one side of the card, narrow beams come out from the other side of it (Picture 4). Here, too, you can see the light travelling in straight lines.

Summary
- Light travels in straight lines.
- A beam of light is a thick stream of bright light.

Weblink: www.curriculumvisions.com

Where sunlight reaches

When sunlight reaches something it makes it bright. This is called illumination. Other places lie in shadow.

So far we have seen that light starts out at a source. The Sun is a source. A torch, a headlamp and a street light are also sources of light. We have also found that light travels in straight lines, but what happens next?

When light reaches something it lights it up. We say that the light has lit it up, or **ILLUMINATED** it.

Blocking out the light

Sunshine travels in straight lines. How does this affect what we see? Look at Picture 1. Notice how bright some things are. These are places where the sunlight can reach directly. Now see how dark it is in other parts of the picture. This is where direct sunlight has been blocked by the wall or the arch. Places which do not get direct sunlight are darker. We say they are in **SHADE**.

Shadows and silhouettes

In fact, if you stand in the shade, you can see darkness by looking towards the light as well as away from it. For example, when you stand in the shade of a tree lit by the Sun you see two dark shapes (Picture 2).

If you first stand with your back to the tree and look at the ground, you will see a dark shape on the ground. This is the tree's **SHADOW**.

If you now turn around and face the tree, you will see the dark shape of the tree

▲ **(Picture 1) Places in direct sunlight and places in shadow. The sharp edge between the two shows that light travels in straight lines.**

against the bright sky. This is called the tree's **SILHOUETTE**.

Both the shadow and the silhouette give you a dark, 'flat' view of the tree. These views have no detail.

12

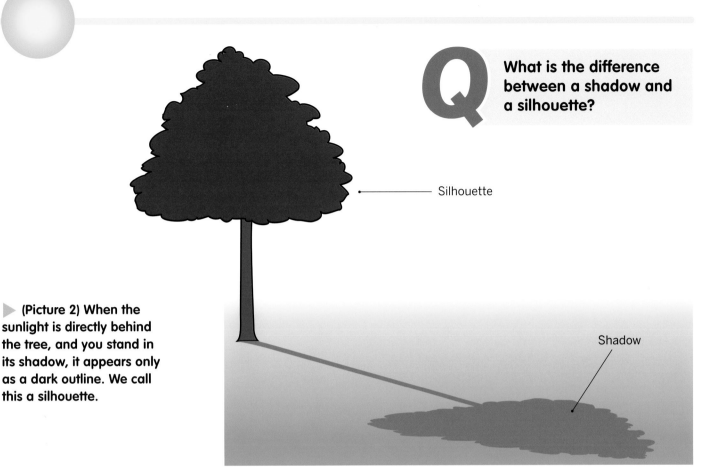

Q What is the difference between a shadow and a silhouette?

Silhouette

Shadow

▶ (Picture 2) When the sunlight is directly behind the tree, and you stand in its shadow, it appears only as a dark outline. We call this a silhouette.

Where to look for shadows

Shadows are all around us. There are lots of shadows when the Sun is shining brightly. Walk along a city street and you will often see one side of the street in sunlight while the other side is in shadow (Picture 3). Lights indoors also cast shadows.

Summary
• Places light cannot reach are in shadow.
• There are a lot of shadows when the Sun is shining brightly.

▶ (Picture 3) When you walk along a street in sunlight, you can see a clear line between the places in sunlight (left) and the places in shadow (right).

13

Shadows that grow and shrink

Shadows change their size as they move closer to or farther from the source of light.

If you look behind anything that blocks out light, you will find a much dimmer area. This is called a shadow. Everything inside the shadow is darker than the surroundings.

Shadows from a beam of light

A torch makes a narrow beam of light and is good for showing what shadows are like.

If you place something in the way of a torch beam, and look at its shadow on a screen or a wall in a dark room, the shadow will be equally dark all over.

In Picture 1, a cardboard owl has been used to make a shadow. The shadow is the dark area on the wall.

Notice that the shadow is the same shape as the owl and that it has a very sharp edge to it.

The way to make shadows move, as in shadow plays, is shown in Picture 2.

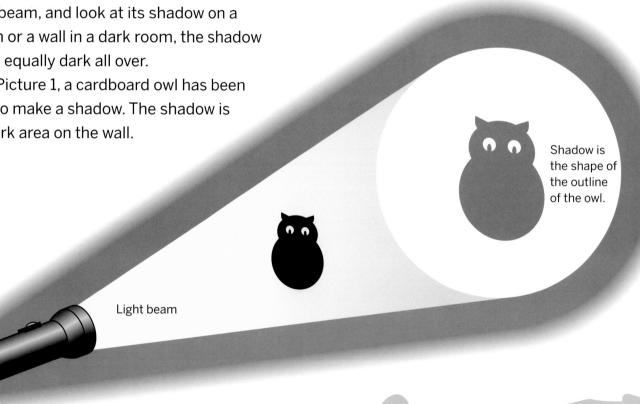

Shadow is the shape of the outline of the owl.

Torch

Light beam

▲ (Picture 1) The shadow is the dark area behind the object.

▶ (Picture 2) You can make your shadows move if you use cutout models supported by wires.

Weblink: www.curriculumvisions.com

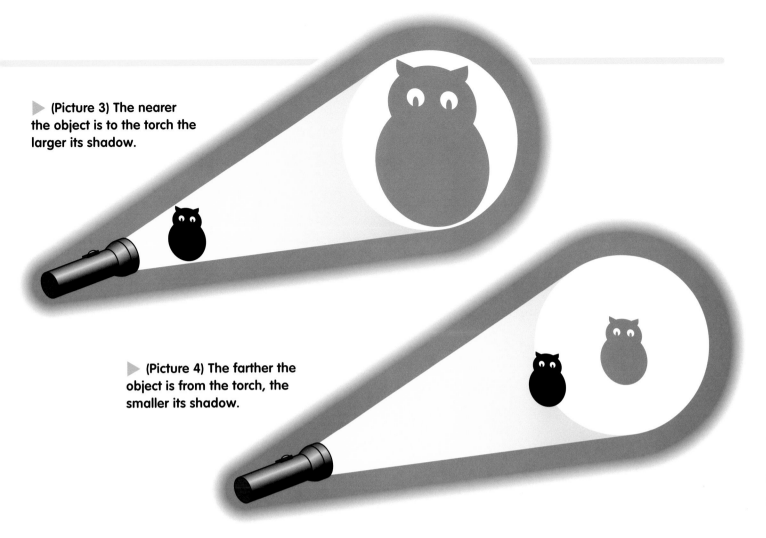

▶ (Picture 3) The nearer the object is to the torch the larger its shadow.

▶ (Picture 4) The farther the object is from the torch, the smaller its shadow.

The size of a shadow

In Picture 3, the owl is close to the torch and the shadow is very large.

In Picture 4, the owl has been moved farther away from the torch. The shadow is now only a little larger than the owl.

▼ (Picture 5) The hand makes a shadow of its own. It is also partly in the shadow of the owl.

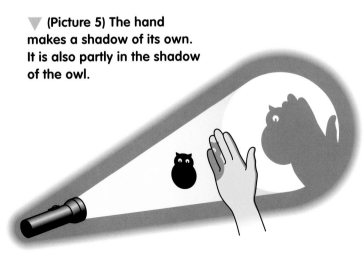

Where is the shadow?

A shadow is the place behind an object where the light has been blocked out.

If you put your hand anywhere behind the owl, then you can watch your hand pass through the torchlight and into the darkness of the shadow of the owl (Picture 5).

Q In a shadow play, you want to make the owl appear to get smaller. Do you move the owl closer to the wall or to the torch?

Summary
- A shadow is the dark area behind an object.
- Shadows are equally dark all over.
- Shadows change size as the object is moved.

Weblink: www.curriculumvisions.com

Shadows change direction

When the source of light moves, the shadows it makes change length and direction.

Have you ever looked at the way your shadow moves? If you stand in a room with only a single light (Picture 1), you can notice these things about your shadow:

▶ That your shadow always faces away from the light.

▶ That your shadow changes direction as you move about the room.

▶ That your shadow begins at your feet, and then spreads out across the floor (and sometimes up the wall).

▶ That your shadow is longer, the farther you stand from the light.

When you are almost beneath the light, your shadow is squashed up; but as you move away from the light, your shadow becomes drawn out. In between, there is a place where your shadow looks about the same length as yourself.

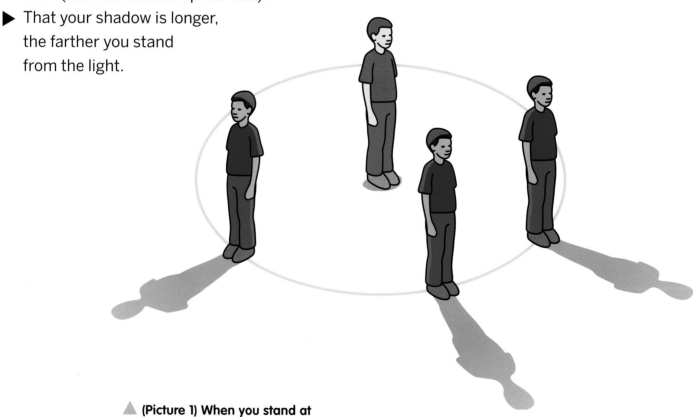

▲ (Picture 1) When you stand at various distances from a single source of light, your shadow changes shape and direction.

Weblink: www.curriculumvisions.com

Q If you had three lights on in the room, how many shadows of yourself would there be?

▼ ▶ **(Picture 2) When the light is lower, your shadow becomes longer.**

Lower light

What happens when the light is lower? Picture 2 shows some of the answers. Notice that compared to Picture 1, the shadows are all longer – except for the one under the light. Otherwise, the directions of the shadows stay the same. You might like to try this out for yourself.

Summary
- Shadows become longer the lower the angle of the light.
- Shadows become more squashed up when the light is overhead.
- Shadows always face away from the source of the light.

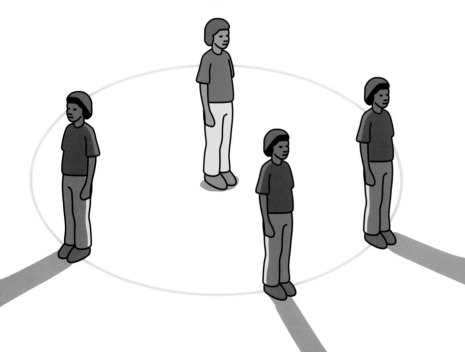

Weblink: www.curriculumvisions.com

Sundials

The Sun is in different parts of the sky at different times during the day. We can trace the changes this brings and use them to tell the time.

Have you noticed that your shadow changes length with the time of day and the time of the year?

Each day the Sun is at a low angle at sunrise, rises to its highest by midday and then sinks down to disappear at sunset* (Picture 1). But there are also changes due to the seasons.

▲ (Picture 2) In the winter, when the angle of the Sun is low in the sky, the shadows are long.

Change by season

In winter, the Sun is always low in the sky, and so the shadows are always long, even at midday (Picture 2). In summer, the Sun quickly rises high in the sky and the shadows are much shorter (Picture 3).

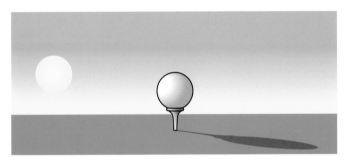

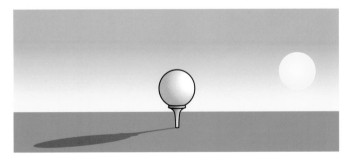

▲ (Picture 1) Shadows cast across the ground are longer at the beginning and the end of the day than they are at midday.

(*For more on this see the *Science@School* book *5E Earth and beyond*)

▶ (Picture 3) In the summer, when the angle of the Sun is high in the sky, the shadows are short.

Daily changes

You can investigate the daily change in shadow direction and length by using a stick placed upright on open ground. If you place the stick on a lawn, you can mark the length and position of the shadow by using a trail of sand. If you place the stick in a sand pit, you can mark the changes with pebbles (Picture 4).

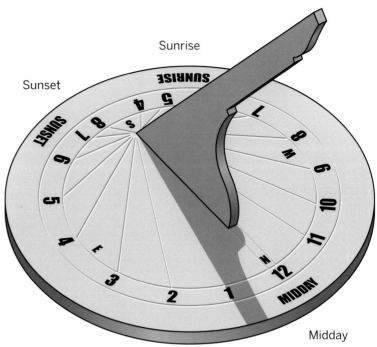

Sunset   Sunrise

Midday

▲ (Picture 5) This sundial is marked in hours.

▼ (Picture 4) The length of a shadow from a stick being measured each hour. In this case a stone, and the time in pebbles, are used as markers.

Sundials

Because the shadows change in a reliable way, you can use them to tell the time (so long as the Sun is shining). In the past, people told the time this way by making an instrument called a **SUNDIAL** (Picture 5).

Sundials can be made to be flat, or upright on a wall.

You can make a simple sundial by folding over a card so that one part stands upright. Then stick it to a circle of cardboard.

Q When can't you use a sundial to tell the time?

Summary
- As the Sun moves, the shadows move too.
- Sundials use moving shadows to tell the time.

Weblink: www.curriculumvisions.com

Getting rid of shadows

Shadows can be a nuisance. You can get rid of them by using many lights, or just a piece of card.

Whenever you have just one source of light you will always have shadows. In some cases, shadows can be a problem (Picture 1). So how can we get rid of shadows?

Adding sources of light

In Picture 2, you can see what happens if we use more than one source of light.

The top diagram (**A**) shows a view from above of the shadow of a mug cast by a single bulb. The middle picture (**B**) shows that when we use two bulbs, the shadow of the mug shrinks. In the bottom picture (**C**), placing the mug between the bulbs completely gets rid of the shadow.

(Picture 1) It can be difficult to read a book if it is in the strong shadow cast by a single room light.

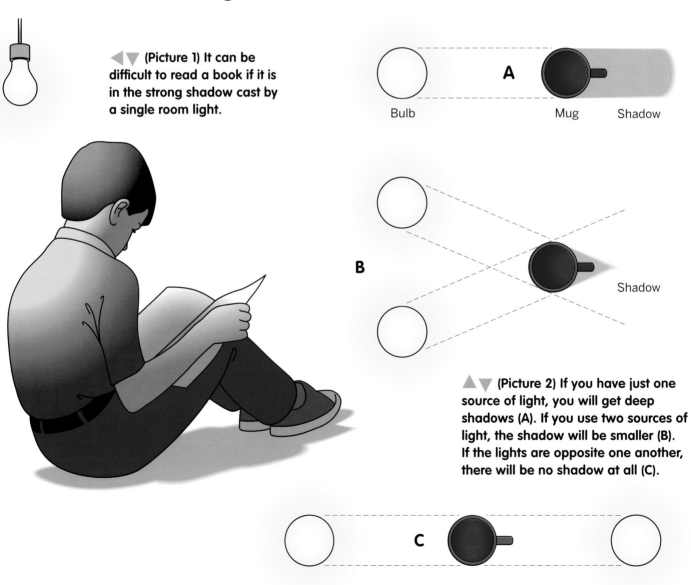

Bulb   Mug   Shadow

A

B

Shadow

(Picture 2) If you have just one source of light, you will get deep shadows (A). If you use two sources of light, the shadow will be smaller (B). If the lights are opposite one another, there will be no shadow at all (C).

C

Weblink: www.curriculumvisions.com

This is a very important idea, and used in places such as a hospital operating theatre (Picture 3).

Adding light-bouncing card

If all you want to do is to make the shadow weaker, you do not need extra bulbs. Instead, all you need is white card or shiny foil (Picture 4). The card or foil must be placed so that it faces the bulb.

To see how this works, think of a ball as part of a beam of light (Picture 5). When you throw the ball against a wall it is like a beam of light striking the card or foil.

When the ball hits the wall, it bounces back. This is what happens when light hits the card or foil. This light bouncing is called **REFLECTION**.

The lighter the colour of the card, the more it will reflect light, whereas the darker the card, the less light will be reflected.

▼ **(Picture 3) When it is important to get rid of all shadows, people use many lights, as, for example, in this operating theatre in a hospital.**

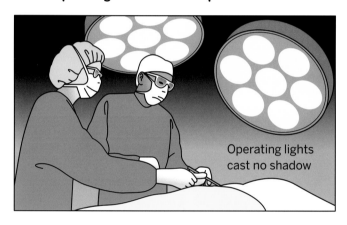

Operating lights cast no shadow

▼ **(Picture 4) Shadows can be lightened by using a reflecting card.**

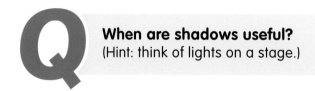

Q **When are shadows useful?**
(Hint: think of lights on a stage.)

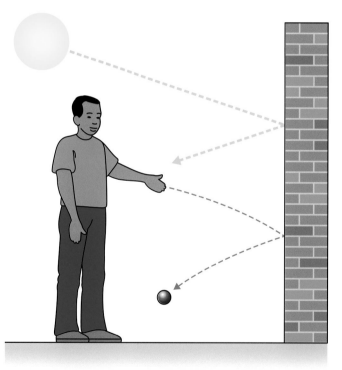

▲ **(Picture 5) Light bounces from surfaces just as a ball bounces from a wall.**

Summary

- **Shadows can be removed by using many lights.**
- **Shadows can be lessened by using light-bouncing materials.**

Weblink: www.curriculumvisions.com

Letting light through

Some objects let light through. When these objects are perfectly clear, we call them transparent. Otherwise we call them translucent.

Most things block the light completely so that it is dark behind them. A substance that blocks the light is called **OPAQUE**. But some materials let light through. If you can see through something clearly it is called **TRANSPARENT** (Picture 1).

Air is transparent. A sheet of glass is transparent. Other transparent substances include water (Picture 2) and some kinds of plastic.

Even transparent objects still block out a little light. In general, the thicker the object is, the more light is blocked. This is why you can see through a glass of water but not to the bottom of an ocean.

Translucent

A few materials let some light through but not as much as if they were transparent. Greaseproof paper is an example of this. Thin materials, such as roller blinds on windows and cloth handkerchiefs, let some light through.

You cannot see as clearly through this kind of material as you could through something that is transparent, but a bright light, like a projector, can send light right through it (Picture 3). These materials are called **TRANSLUCENT**.

▼ (Picture 1) You can see through the plastic used for the case of this telephone, so it is transparent. The girl's skin and hair, her red headband and the parts inside the telephone are opaque.

▲ (Picture 2) Water is transparent. You can clearly see the bottom of this bowl.

▼ (Picture 3) Greaseproof paper is a translucent material. This is why you can use it to make shadow plays.

Weblink: www.curriculumvisions.com

Filters

Some materials will just block out some parts of the light. If you hold a piece of red tissue paper in front of your eyes, you will be able to see clearly through it. But the only colour that comes through is red. This type of material is called a **FILTER**.

Coloured glass will only let through light that is the same colour as the glass. You can see this in some churches that have **STAINED GLASS WINDOWS** (Picture 4). You can make your own stained glass window using tissue paper.

Filters are used in TV studios, theatres and concert halls to give special coloured effects. They are also used in traffic lights (Picture 5).

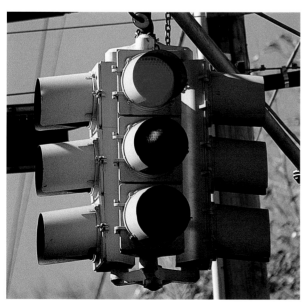

▲▶ (Picture 4) Stained glass is a filter. You can make filters that look like stained glass from tissue paper.

Q If you wanted to use a normal bulb to cast a blue light, what colour filters would you use?

◀ (Picture 5) Traffic lights are examples of filters. Inside each light there is an ordinary white bulb. To get the red, amber and green lights, coloured filters are placed in front of each bulb.

Summary
- A material that lets through light is called transparent.
- A material that blocks light is called opaque.
- A material that lets through some light is called translucent.
- A material that lets through only light of one colour is called a filter.

Weblink: www.curriculumvisions.com

Index

Curriculum Visions

Science@School

Teacher's Guide

There is a Teacher's Guide to accompany this book, available only from the publisher.

There's much more online including videos

You will find multimedia resources covering this and ALL 37 QCA Key Stage 1 and 2 science units as well as history, geography, religion, MFL, maths, music, spelling and more at:

www.CurriculumVisions.com

(Subscription required)

A CVP Book
This second edition © Atlantic Europe Publishing 2011

First edition 2002. First reprint 2004. Second reprint 2006.

The right of Brian Knapp to be identified as the author of this work has been asserted by him in accordance with the Copyright, Designs and Patents Act 1988.

All rights reserved. No part of this publication may be reproduced, stored in a retrieval system, or transmitted in any form or by any means, electronic, mechanical, photocopying, recording or otherwise, without prior permission of the copyright holder.

Author
Brian Knapp, BSc, PhD
Educational Consultant
Peter Riley, BSc, C Biol, MI Biol, PGCE
Art Director
Duncan McCrae, BSc

Senior Designer
Adele Humphries, BA, PGCE
Editor
Lisa Magloff, MA
Illustrations
David Woodroffe
Designed and produced by
Atlantic Europe Publishing
Printed in China by
WKT Company Ltd

Volume 3F Light and shadows 2nd Edition
– Curriculum Visions Science@School
A CIP record for this book is available from the British Library.
Paperback ISBN 978 1 86214 680 8

Picture credits
All photographs are from the Earthscape and ShutterStock collections.

This product is manufactured from sustainable managed forests. For every tree cut down at least one more is planted.